Collected Poems

of

Kenneth P. Firnstahl

Young Man Grown Old

A Poet's Journey Home

Collected Poems

of

Kenneth P. Firnstahl

from 1942–2013

ISBN 979-8-218-46341-0 (hard cover edition)
ISBN 979-8-218-46342-7 (soft cover edition)
Library of Congress Control Number 9798218463410

Book Design by Paul Nylander | Illustrada Design

Front cover: Ken Firnstahl, age 18, shortly before heading to boot camp.
Back cover: Ken Firnstahl about sixteen years old.

Published by McCutcheon/Kelley
Andover, Minnesota

This book is dedicated to my mother, Mary, who adored my father as he did her. Many of the poems were written about her, his love and life with her and the great loss he endured after she had passed on.

A very special thanks to the renowned Norton Stillman, for his help and kindness in getting my father's book published and most notably his friendship.

Special gratitude for Paul Nylander, on his professionalism, creativity, and patience, in making this book exactly what we wanted.

Thank you to my brother, Jeff Firnstahl and sister, Janice Holth, for their financial support.

—Ken's Daughter
MaryJo Kelley

Foreword

Kierkegaard said, "Drink from your own well." He meant that each of us has an individual source for our best work and that we should not ignore it. Ken, through his poems, has given us a picture of his life, "his own well."

Where does his poetry come from? From his experiences in wartime, his sense of humor, his respect for good books, his devotion to family, his feelings of aging and loss, and his love of nature.

Dylan Thomas said, "My poetry is the record of my individual struggle from darkness toward some measure of light." In his poems, Ken "paints words to lite the starry night." He seeks to awaken our souls to the beauty of nature and God's Spirit.

In this collection of Ken's works the reader experiences the full range of Ken's poetic voice. May it be enjoyed as it is explored, one poem at a time.

—David Holth

EARLY YEARS – 1942

*First Poems written during his service in
the US Navy, WWII*

A Letter

Funny thing a letter,
You don't know where to start,
Specially if you want your girl
To know what's in your heart.

Make it just a bit poetic
If your girls the type,
For you've got to be romantic
If the letter's to be right.

Now add a bit of starlight
And the color of the moon,
How perfect things could be
If we could share them soon.

Now that's my type of letter,
Every word of it is true,
Just as God knows in heaven darling,
I love you.

First poem, age 18

A Bit More Shy

For as the years they pass me by,
I seem to grow a bit more shy.
For now a girl could wink her eye
And I'm the one to heave a sigh!

I Shall Not Think Of Her

I shall not think of her tonight,
My heart could not withstand;
I shall not think of her tonight,
I have a different plan.

I'll think of her tomorrow,
When the sun is shining bright;
I'll think of her tomorrow,
When the moon is not in sight.

The night has lost its' beauty,
The star light hurts my eyes;
Maybe my tears are burning,
One knows when his heart dies.

So Far Away From Home

We wandered through the lanes at night,
And danced beneath the moon.
We laughed at flying fireflies,
And sang our favorite tune.

Our hearts flew up upon a star,
And sailed across the sky.
The world seemed bright and new again,
A prize for you and I.

I hoped this night would never end,
The moon would stay on high.
Your sparkling laughter never cease,
Your beauty never die.

I hoped that I would never wake,
To find myself alone.
For dreams like these should never be,
So far away from home.

Your Letter

Your letter just arrived today,
I have it near my heart.
And thus the world came down to me,
And left its richest part.

I guess its slightly crumpled now,
I've read it many times.
Funny how close you seem to me
Each time I read those lines.

It seems that you appeared to me,
And then I heard you speak,
As though a golden harp were touched,
So beautiful, I did weep.

I kissed your hand and kissed your cheek,
And then you fled from sight,
I'll find you in my dreams again,
I'll dream of you tonight.

You can call me sentimental,
Yes, a dreamer that is true.
Yet how could I compose a poem
Without a girl like you.

The Rain That Poured

The rain that poured outside my door,
Brings back the days when I was four,
Why I'd wade in all the puddles deep—
And water in my shoes did seep.

My toy boat sailed in every stream,
And of the ocean I did dream.
As every crack of thunder roared—
It was my guns that had just scored.

Far from it be, that I some day,
Should sail away from Frisco's Bay.
Adventure to some unknown land—
A beach of coral and white sand.

It's not quite like one dreams at four,
Your youth grows sober during times of war.
There's not much thrill at the crack of a gun,
When there's blood stained decks from someone's son.

So such is war, it has to be;
If were to keep our country free.
So if your heart in heavy and sore,
Well, just dream of the days when you were four.

Draw Not Thy Sword

Draw not thy sword in anger Sir,
Draw not thy sword in fear,
but draw your sword to cut the cake,
a gesture of good cheer.

Three mighty years of service Sir,
Beneath old Glory past.
To know we served her well,
Is all the credit asked.

So cut the cake dear Captain,
This honor we implore,
To set us on a new year—
And the ending of the war.

I Have Often Tried

I have often tried to write a poem
About a world of peace,
About a sky that's always blue,
A land where trouble cease.

But each time I'd start to write
My pen would strive in vain.
You see my heart is not in tune
With words that are not plain.

I'd have to write of war and strife
Of things my eyes have seen.
A sky that's dark with gun smoke
A land where hearts are lean.

I'd have to write of shattered dreams,
Of mothers who've lost their sons.
A face with eyes that cannot see,
The cries of little ones.

I'd rather write of love and spring,
A poem about the fall.
For if one must write of war and strife,
Best not write at all.

To Hold Your Hand

To hold your hand again in mine,
To watch the smile upon your face,
To know that you are just with me,
I'd give the world and all its' race.

I'd work and strive for you a home,
A home that we can call our own.
A little place beside a brook,
A garden of flowers at which to look.

When our home is all complete,
We'd have a child for us to keep.
I know no father more proud could be
Of a child you had borne for me.

Then that time when we grow old,
Our home in vines has then enfold
I'll hold your hand again in mine,
My life could be no more sublime.

POEMS ABOUT FAMILY

David Holth (1950–2006)

He dies, husband, father, doctor, scholar
No doubt one of the finest men
To grace the Earth.

Jan cried, rivers of tears like falling
Rain, spilling o're the heart—submerging
Her soul in sorrow.

People mourned, friends, patients,
Those who knew little of him,
Felt a great loss.

So what did he leave? Certainly the warm
Memories of him. Yes, and blessings
He left all of us. The privilege of
Knowing him. The blessing to have
Lived with him. Count them and say
An Ave.

For who among us has lived as
The Holy Scripture teach? David did.
Never a foul word from him.
I count his blessings and how he
Improved my life and yes,
I cried.

My love,
Ken Firnstahl

Elizabeth

Lovely May . . . like a new babe
    On the wings of spring
Burst forth upon a new day . . .
    A morn my Elizabeth Ann did bring.

Trees with new born buds
    Laced with droplets of dew . . .
Await dawns shower of sun
    To hail Elizabeth . . . my little one.

Elizabeth . . . like the morn of birth
    Bright new life to start.
Brought with her the morning sun
    And placed its light within my heart.

She is spring . . . its blossoming
    Flowers with dew drops wet.
More than this . . . she is love locked
    In my soul . . . never to forget.

Grandpa Ken

Kay

She died—left her tired worn body
And reached to catch a star.
To sail beyond the fringe of Earth
To heaven's gate afar.

Elated that her soul lives on
A bless'd reality
Now a spirit of celestial joy
With immortality.

Kimmy

Oh! Blossoming youth at dawn of life.
Looks down the yawning throat of beckoning earth,
The old worn angry earth. It's well you have fear,
She's young and strong in her fourteenth year.

Now at the foot of life's high mountain,
Peers up at the snowy cloud hooded peak.
She will scale your slopes to stand at your crest,
Where eagles sore above their nest.

Trained like a Spartan through books of wisdom
Her Thermopylae of life ahead.
With a shield of knowledge, love and faith,
Her spear tipped with truth and God's holy grace.

This modern Joan of Ark, glorious in her shining armor,
Vanquishing foes astride her mighty stead,
Dismounts to pray on bended knee,
Her triumph blessed, in God succeed.

This is my beautiful Kimmy who challenges life.
This brave young girl, with ringlet curls,
Great love for her parents and handsome
Young brother, sparing some I pray
For her adoring grandfather.

Laura

This little girl with golden curls,
This lovely child with turned up nose;
Takes my hand on cabin road—
To talk of Indians, bears and wolves,
Then climbs upon my lap to doze.

Soon a slender lovely girl—
Willowy form with style and grace,
Perfumes hair, ribbon and lace
A brilliant lady of poise and charm;
Confident and assured her special place.

Yet all these sterling attributes
Pale compared to love she gives—
Now guides me and leads the way
This precious child with pleasing aura
The child I love, my darling Laura.

Grandpa Ken

Little Renae

What words describe this lovely face,
Or adjectives reveal such grace.
Compare her to the morning sun,
Her eyes to starlight, hair gold spun.

Oh! Sages tell of songs unsung,
Of master painting yet begun.
What clue to her dear Lord have I?
The answer came from out the sky,
A single blue bird winged my way,
Caroling sweetly of Little Renae.

Grandpa Ken

Mary

A mist about my eyes,
When reading , "who is she?"
Mindful of a lady close to me,
Now in lonely grave at rest.

I dwell on her often,
She is not far. No further
Than my grieving heart. She
Remains close to me, I love her so.

She's with me at close of day,
She's with me at rising sun.
She's at my side as I kneel in prayer,
She holds my hand to guide me there.

She is the sun, the blossoming flowers,
She is the end of day and setting sun.
She is my Mary, and as for me—
She is always and ever my only one.

Mary Firnstahl, My Wife

I'm alone, Mary my wife in a nursing home.
Our house is silent, all I hear is the wind
And weird sounds the wind creates.
I search for comfort, there is none.

The rooms I loved, have faded into obscurity
No longer friendly, instead cold, dissident.
I dwell on our great memories and love,
Our beautiful family—'tho silent.

I dwell on our before dinner cocktail.
What a time of closure and peace.
We discussed books and poetry—
She was always ready to compliment.

Each day I feel more alone—
A sadness with her in my thoughts.
The phone is silent, I feel helpless.
I ask for God's help, God knows
My sadness, thus I pray!

Mary Jo

Mary Jo like a graceful bird in flight
Swoops in our home to touch our hearts.
Chirps and chatters the latest news,
Then flutters away with dove like coos.

Enthused with life, opinions fly
Sturdy convictions she'll not deny.
If you should question, prepare to fight,
The melee may last well into the night.

One shan't dispute her active mind, or
Physical beauty through disciplined minded
Her fervor for life deflecting its knocks,
Glamour compared to Ms.Courtney Cox.

Though times may pass, memory lapse,
She remains like a Rembrandt painting,
Yet explain if you will from our minds
Lock box, who pray thee is
Ms.Courtney Cox?

Renae

Crushing pain unrelenting upon her flight.
Lies hidden in shadows of sullen heart.
A part of her remains thru time
Her slender hand enclosed in mine.

She joins me at dusk of day,
To wile the evening hours away.
Chopin with a glass of wine,
A book of verse, (pray none of mine).

She laughs at drinking cheap Chablis
Pours Kendall Jackson just for me.
Discusses Bach and jazz at ease,
A special toast—Jane Austin please.

Yet mom and dad, wait till you hear,
I hold front row, center, Heaven's seats
The three of us to applaud and share,
God's Heavenly chorus performing there.

Sonnet to My Daughter Patty

A love of a father be more rare
The love of a mother always there.
My life amid December snows
My days be past the best.
Her gentle heart dispels
The sorrow near life's end.
Her Christ like love,
Most tender friend.
She warms my heart,
In sunlit glow,
Her deep respect and loving care
Lifts my tired soul.
Her love borne on spring like air
My beautiful daughter of golden hair.

Love,
Dad

Tanya

Who is Tanya you ask?
Like a lovely portrait perhaps,
With the gracious beauty of a Chopin Nocturne—
And the rays of the morning sun.

Tell more of Tanya?
Her serenity of the evening star,
Her delight of a Christmas carol,
Her freshness of a morning in June.

What more or Tanya?
She is love, God's love,
God's gift to us all,
My aging heart now young as sunlit May,
Tanya, dear grandchild, kissed me this day.

Grandpa Ken

Tiffani's Wedding

An angel at the alter glows
As bathed in morning's rising sun.
A radiant vision in flowing white,
Sacred music accents her grace
Candles soft light, her lovely face.

Fragrant flowers held in hand,
Pale to beauty of this bride,
Adoring groom at her side,
Clasps her hand in righteous pride.

Divinely wed, with heavenly smile,
She walks in beauty down the isle,
Paused to nod, then passed me by,
Thus I'll love her 'til I die.

'Tis then I breathe a gentle sigh,
Her wedding Mass offered in glory on high,
That God will hold them in loving embrace,
And one day they behold his face.

Love, Grandpa Ken

Tiger

You seldom hear a word bestowed,
Upon the family dog.
Or epitaph or sonnets versed,
Of love it gives, respect deserved.

Oh! Some will have a special place,
Where dogs are put away.
And others just a shallow grave,
Their last respects to pay.

For me I want to stroke his back,
Softly speak to him,
Kiss his noble furry head,
Before his final bed.

Tell how much we love him,
What a fine dog he has been.
My world will be much less, for me
Without my friend, and grief so deep,
The day they put our Tiger to sleep.

But then again, should I go first,
My Tiger left behind.
Perhaps he'll wail a tear for me,
A mournful howl, his special kind.

YOUNG KEN FIRNSTAHL.

OTTO FIRNSTAHL, KEN'S FATHER.

KEN FIRNSTAHL 18 YEARS OLD.

NAVY DISCHARGE. KEN ON THE RIGHT.

KEN STANDING BY THE FAMILY CAR.

ROBERT (KEN'S BROTHER, LEFT) AND FRIENDS, THEN
SISTERS MARGARET, CATHARINE, AND KEN (FAR RIGHT).

KEN (SECOND FROM RIGHT) HANGING OUT WITH FRIENDS.

KEN AND MARY OUT FOR THE EVENING.

WEDDING NIGHT.

(CLOCKWISE FROM LEFT) JANICE, PATRICIA, MARY, KEN, MARYJO, JEFF, AND RENAÉ. ABOUT 1983.

(CLOCKWISE FROM LEFT) PATRICIA, JEFF, JANICE, MARYJO, MARY, AND KEN, IN 2000.

DREAM HOME ON RICE CREEK TERRACE.

HOME VIEWED FROM RICE CREEK.

RENAÉ AND KEN HEADING TO CANADA FOR A FISHING
TRIP IN 1980.

KEN AT THE FAMILY CABIN ON LAKE ROOSEVELT.

FIFTIETH WEDDING ANNIVERSARY CELEBRATION.

PORTRAIT OF MARY AND KEN.

LATER YEARS

Poems about Faith, Family, Life and Love

A Father's Thoughts

I thought of her today at Mass,
I thought of her in silent grave
Behind the church where in I kneel.
I thought of her and where she slept,
The tomb with timeless secrets kept,
I thought of her today—and wept.

A Hug For Me

Her image glows with beauty
Gazes from the picture on the wall.
Touching my heart,
My soul yet weeps.

She's no longer with us.
Her body nine years beneath headstone
And earth. Only her picture to hold and see.
Please God, (of all love) give her a hug for me.

In memory of his daughter Renae.

A Man I Remain

Thankful for my place in life,
A gift from God my lovely wife,
The Children she had borne for me
Healthy, normal and drug free.

The many tests and strife of life,
The foolishness you fail to hide.
To strive to live in properness,
At home, at work in God confide.

For all that I am thankful for,
The many blessings my Lord you bring,
There's one I haply, haply sing
A man I remain, there's no ear ring.

A Sorry Tail

His trousers hang slack
As seen from the back,
With excessive pounds on his hips and gut.
What ever happened to his once proud butt?

It's a sorry tale that this should pass
The old man like most
Has lost his ass!

A Time of Political Correctness

I pan for truth, the nuggets of gold
I sift the minds of scholars.
Books stacked high about my world
Pages worn, soiled for answers yet untold.

Theology, philosophy, history, poetry
My eyes grow dim, can I write it
Before my time? Lift the ever pressing
Burden, free the tired soul!

Can I rest when truth is accepted?
'Tis folly to expect even repartee with
Professors, clergy, fellow associates
Serious recourse evades me.

My books fail the test, this horror.
Schools, universities exclude all of it.
Thus standing at the shrine of truth
This lonely figure, don't let it fall.

Accumulating Years

Accumulating years lie heavily
On the frailty of human spirit,
Settling on the breath of life.
Retaining it's grief and pain
It's joys and love.

The strong, perhaps retain more time,
Still the weight of days extract
A toll, the body tires and slows,
Welcoming rest and time to reflect.

Heavens celestial doors loom closer,
You grasp at stars to slow the pace,
And pray to catch your breath, survive
For yet another day.

Your final days, like good aged wine,
Fermented with wisdom and love, take
Time to sip and savor the loveliness
Of life's breath. Then grasp the
Hand of God and toast approaching death.

Adoration Hour

Humbly you enter His sanctuary, where
Christ dwells within the Blessed Sacrament.
You kneel, bowing deeply in the sacred silence,
Then take your place to spend your chosen
Hour with Christ.

How privileged you are that come to visit
Christ this late hour. The discipline to
Travel this dark night is tempered with
An angel's voice, "you did not arrive alone,
Christ journeyed with you."

You clasp a book of prayers, yet fail to open.
Spellbound in the blessed silence, you listen!
Listen! You hear it! It's everywhere,
The Word! The Word of God, God's Holy Word.

You feel God's comforting presence, His solemn
Serenity, his healing peace, his boundless love,
You sense his saints bowed in adoration
About his sacred Host. Our Holy Mother
In prayer there, the fragrance of lilacs
In the air.

How lovely is your dwelling place my Lord, how
Quickly the precious time passes. The quiet
Hour a gift to caress the soul, begs
Introspect and prayer, refreshes the spirit—
Knowing Christ is there.

Advice for the Aspiring Scholar

Oh! That you breathe life into the silent centuries past,
Excite the fallow minds to ages lost.
Awaken the quiet graves to hear once more,
The thinkers, philosophers, poets, sadly long ignored.

Stir and shake classroom routine,
Open windows that thoughts of great minds
Long forgotten may enter, rattle, inspire,
Imaginations of all that dare listen.

The brilliant melancholy, Samuel Johnson
May spur your interests and interpretation of
Shakespeare. What of Petrarch? Rousseau?
Montaigne? The verse of Ben Johnson
And Goethe?

Loose the headstones of Shiller, Hegel.
Call up Rabelais and the exciting Germaine.
DeSteal. Look to books on Caesar, Napoleon.
Peruse the writings of Socrates, Plato,
Seneca.

Ah! Socrates, 400 B.C. spoke of rights
And wrongs. Preached justice, morals,
Piety, love and the soul. Cognate of
Christ. Best disguise his presence,
And hold the hemlock.

Cajole with rotund Henry VIII while
Maintaining your head. Observe the
Sly Woolsey scheme. Reach out to
Scholarly Thomas Moore and
The intellect of Erasmus.

Train with Spartans at Thermopylae,
Take time for artists and poets
Of Athens. Look to Homer as to
The culture of Greece and Egypt,
Civilizations dawning.

Review with Samuel Johnson,
Enjoy a pint of ale with the doctor,
His friends Boswell and Diderot in
His favorite English pub. Rejoice,
You have started your journey
From student to scholar.

You have pricked the bubble of
Knowledge, sans p.c. Most frightening,
You will have uncovered truth.

After Heart Surgery

I've been well long enough,
Kind nature has tired, depleted.
'Tis time for age to foul the mind
Ravage the once strong spirit.

Time to stumble, lose the way.
Time for disregard, go unheeded, ignored.
Time to accept harsh terms,
You're old, you're eccentric, be silent.

Spirits of fermenti to soothe.
Books and music solace intellect
Unshared to quiet loneliness,
The grave awaits as final bed.

Yet for it all, I've reached old age
Gathered wisdom unto myself
Look back on honored goals.
Still a comfort as old age unfolds.

Age of Winter

My life has reached the winter of time,
Accompanying yellow leaves
Lie buried 'neath the crusty snows of age.

What dreams unfold with final breath
Now stilled. Old age, it's wisdom and propriety
Has no dominion ore' fragile mortality

Ancient Rome Revisited

Now is the late term of life,
All the good spirits surrounding me,
I labor for plain speech that
May enlighten or direct. Yet more often
Stingingly considered a relic with
Opinions, wisdom, non-cogent.

It may be time to pursue eccentricities,
The accepted stamp of age.
Time to practice curmudgenry.
Hand maiden to elder years.
Withdraw to a dark corner
And doze the time away.

Yet life's angel enfolds me
With her comforting wings
Whispers not a benediction to death
But holds off the inevitable dreamless
Sleep—to rage and weep societies decent.

I lived when humans were turned to soap.
Choice, sentenced millions of unborn
Children to violent death.
Needles supplied to drug addicts,
Deceit, adultery, violence condones.
Condoms distributed to out children,
God expelled from public schools,
Christmas denied, prayer forbidden.

The fading sunrise of life looks
On a descending moral compass
Of our nation
Once like a great shooting star,
Only to extinguish, falter in
Foul decay.

Thus I savor days past with all
Its glory, joy, sadness and grief.
Days not perfect, but secure
In understanding right from wrong.

Just as Gibbon had in 1764, I too
Sit among the ruins of the capital
At close of day on the steps of the
Temple of Jupiter, listening to
Franciscan Friar sing evening
Vespers and pray God set our
Nation right. That Franklin,
Jefferson, Madison will prevail and
America restored. Forbid we sit
Among these ruins to tell sad
Stories on the death of morality.

Those left of euphoria, do not despair.
Take heart, it is only musing
Of an elderly citizen, who served an loves this country
With no wish to impugn. Therefore if you
Grieve—no need to shed tears.
America does not care the majority
No out rage. I pray they would!
If you have prayed—consider prayer again.

And if Thou Wilt, Remember

Grief rides the storm of tragedy,
Coursing and seeking the fragile heart.
We cling together for solace,
Looking to the shoulder of God.

Prayers winging towards heaven
Are the arms that reach out
To caress her soul, and again
We rock her in the cradle of love.

We stand by her grave—a single tree,
Green grass and flowers mark her place.
We listen to the wind rustle the leaves,
And then ever so softly the sound of a
Piano—playing Chopin—as though carried
By a breeze. How could you not
Remember, how could you
Ever forget?

Angel of Love

Age has ravished the once strong spirit.
Now infirmities, pain and lasting discomfort
Are the devout enemies that prey
On him day and night.

His days have emerged from the bright
Sunrise of life, to the now melancholy
Long shadows of dusk. Yet this pale
Light reveals a blessed life.

He looks back through the misty glow of
Past years, with love, love of an angel,
Borne of God, after sixty years of her
Bliss, she had flown high with angels of heaven.

She is now a guardian angel to the man
She loved, he feels her presence and warmth.
She is with him
She holds him, as God holds her, his angel
Of love.

Angel on the Mantle

An angel on their mantle stands,
Flew there the day she took her leave.
Years have past, her sister flown,
Yet the angel on the mantel stands.
Her spirit remains within her home.

Oft times I feel a sullen loss,
That she had left so soon.
The beautiful angel lying abed,
A fading world within her room.

With scholarly poise, poetic mind,
Still abreast of the sporting worlds
Baseball averages, weakness and strength,
On this the child could speak at length.

Now in heaven, hovering above,
I hear the sound of ethereal wings.
Vivaldi, Bach and angels sing
Amidst the chorus of violin,
Conducting from a cloud like mantle
God's special angel, their little girl,
A lovely sight—our Mary Lynn.

Apologies to the Bard

I hath golfed not yet two months
And could perceive no truth in
What hath been said. Whence was it
I hath kept my head down—my left foot planted.
And my swing easy.

My game hath fallen into
Topped shots, fat hits, and poorly putted balls.
That what should accompany an
Aged player—towering drives,
Fairest way shots, accurate, smooth pitches—
I cannot look to have—but instead place much
Foul speech that trippeth from
The tongue. Full of sound and fury
Yet prove nothing—what is't with me
When every ball I hit appalls me so?

It is the short topped hit
From the tee that befalls me
Which oft times assures me first
Shot from same tee.
As I prove no threat to competing
Players, not far along links.

Away with thee long slump.
My golf's but a quest for a straight
Shot, perchance a mulligan—
A prayer that I may hooketh not.

Oh that when I shuffle off that last long ball
It fall gently to a hole in one.
Must give me pause—what dreams
May come—when fellows cheer
Such prowess—there's the respect
To bring serenity to so long life.

Approaching Death

Accumulating years lie heavily
On the frailty of human spirit,
Settling on the breath of life.
Retaining its grief and pain
Its joys and love.

The strong, perhaps retain more time,
Still the weight of days extract
A toll, the body tires and slows,
Welcoming rest and time to reflect.

Heavens celestial doors loom closer,
You grasp at stars to slow the pace,
And pray to catch your breath, survive
For yet another day.

Your final days, like good aged wine,
Fermented with wisdom and love, take
Time to sip and savor the loneliness
Of life's breathe. Then grasp the
Hand of God and toast approaching death.

Art or Plight

Life's vine withers within the Spirit—
My pen near dry writes with fainter soul
The glory of earth and sorrows pain
Remain edged in recesses of memory.

The heart now emptied on pages
Where on I write, splashed across
Legal pads, note and scratch paper.
Thoughts and visions of an elder mind.

Verse on the pangs of war,
Lines on the bliss of love,
Agony of a child's death
Psalms of a aging man.

While youth in the grasp of spring
 Cling together with their griefs and loves
 Look past the lines I write
 Unaware of my art or plight.

Cabin, Night-Music-Moon Lite

Alone in the quiet of the cabin night
A single lamp to shed the darkness
Through the window the lake shimmers
Darkly with a sliver of the moons pale light.

The family abed in peaceful slumber
I sit with London symphony along with
Rachmaninoff and his concerto#2. In thoughtful
Reverie, watching the moon grow larger—
As the music swells.

The Adagio sostonuto begins, I close my eyes as the
Pianist softly touches the keys, soulful strings
Caress the soul, time to dream in ecstasy through
The minutes of artistry, that should never end.

The moon now full, the music so intense, the beauty and
Serenity seeps into your very being. Too soon,
The final crescendo, a secret amore
Or a prayer in music, at heaven's door.

Close of Day

The old man rests on the lake front deck
Surveys the lovely scene below.
His face pressed against the perfumed breath of spring.
He whispers an "Ave", reflecting on the wonders of God.

The sun, ever lowering,
Slants through trees not yet fully leaved.
While shadows lengthen and glow
Extending to the quiet shore.

Relaxed and prepared for sleep
He watches the tired sun slip away
After it's long day leaving a crimson glow
Beyond the far horizon.

Songbirds sing evening vespers,
As dusk's cover shades the earth.
Its pale light outlines an eagle's flight
Winging above tall shadowy pines
Seeking its nest.

The slap of a beaver tail
Echoes across the placid lake
Stirring loons to a series of shrill calls,
This great bird's haunting alarm.

Reluctant to retreat from this solitude for meditation
In the far piney woods he long lingers
For God has revealed a glimpse of heaven
This close of day.

Corpsman's Requiem WWII

Landing craft approaches from sea
It's ramp descends in frothy shell laced water,
Marines scramble down to shore
To no man's land of blood and gore.

"Eternal Father strong to save
For those in peril on land or sea"
Young navy corpsman's deadly combat
Life's saving blood held in hand
While thundering artillery shakes the land.

Boots trample the muddy shore
Sucking deep in blood soaked soil
Helmets float in from oily sea
Eternal Father watch over me.

In coming! In coming! Heads down—
Shells scream and burst in blistering
Gun fire. Corpsman! I'm hit!
My Legs! My legs are gone! Please God!

Hold on! I'm coming, leaves what safety—
Crawls into shell shredded air. Comforts
And aides amid crashing explosions—
A weak voice—Thanks Doc—Thank you—take care!
Eternal Father pray be there!

Fears weds courage, tenuous life crawls thru
Clouds of smoke, spent shell casings, past
Men crouched returning fire, reaches blood
Soaked soil, life fading a marine whispers
Help! Swiftly sulfa compresses applied,
Plasma-morphine-machine guns clatter of
Certain death. Sudden darkness, shells split
The skull, Navy Corpsman collapses across

His wounded patient. "Dona Nobis Pacem."
All is quiet, artillery no longer sound, cries
For help cease. Smoke has cleared. Peace overcomes
Him—a new birth. God holds him—the soul
Rises with angel choirs—the war is over—his
still body yet shields the wounded soldier
on Earth. "Dona Eis Requiem."

*Navy Corpsman suffered the highest mortality rate in the South
Pacific in WWII.*

Days Past

Alone I walk these streets of yore,
The very halls I called my own,
The city was mine, I knew it well
The face, the sound, the shops, the smell.

My peers I pass would tip their hats,
Stop to talk, wish me well.
Pause for coffee, discuss our day
The latest gossip, then flip to pay.

Today these streets seem cold and gray.
Once familiar faces—no more.
Like me no longer looks the same
No friendly greetings cheer my way.

My stride has slowed, my bearing
Less sure. My spirit falters, I
Feel alone. I gaze about then
Start for home. Those days are gone
Forever more.

It was them a vision of grace beheld
A welcome sight to warm my heart.
Brought back a glimpse of youth pray thee,
My lovely bride Mary—smiling at me.

Dusk

Dusk settles on shoulders of the old man,
Remnants of setting sun slip away,
Mindful of the old man's days,
His dimmed vision looks back,
To winters of youth, sunless days,
Childhood romances, heartbreak, a smile.

Recalls life's brief tour on the stage of time,
A call to colors, matrimony, little ones,
Tugging at heart and knees—
Hair grayed, children grown, silent empty rooms,
Discarded toys, memories
Hold a wistful place for these.

A sigh escapes his labored breath,
No eulogy, perhaps a plea on high.
He looks up to where heaven waits,
Arms reaching he calls for grace,
Another day, dear God pray,
The sun to wash to dusk away.

Dusty Age

Dusty age like truth a shadowy image
On life's shrinking stage
Stumbles along on worn ground
Where prints remain of once swift feet.

Eloquent wisdom masked in yellowed
Leaves fall from the full mature
Trees of years—to be swept away
And heard no more.

Tells of truth denied and castigated
Yielding false sympathy and tired love.
Tis time to seek a quiet corner of earth
Wile the silent hours away and
Reach for the hand of God.

Fill My Glass

Oh magical fermented grape that loose the tongue
The poetry and prose it doth extol
Stirs culture from years of yore
Pours pure truth that asks for more.

Genius of ages spring lightly forth—
Refill my glass and hear'th more
Socratic wisdom wings centuries from
A 400B.C. symposium.

Another glass please, my flask be dry
This soothing wine doth comfort senses
Another glass to cheer the heart
'Tis snobbery of grape make'th

Final Harvest

The old man's life 77 years past,
The question remains, how long will he last?
His aching bones predict good reason,
He's entered the unmentionable dying season.

Perhaps a body overhaul would do,
His headlights are dimming, the exhaust
Excessive, the valves are sticking, pistons
Noisy, the clutch is slipping and his
Nose is dripping.

The old man smiled with his diagnosis,
His search for truth leaves a subtle neurosis.
Yet savors the days in the setting sun,
No hurry please for the struggle to come.

His daily prayers on knees are said,
Scholarly books at bedside read.
Enjoys good wine and cigars each day,
Toast his harvest be held at bay.

The apple is red, the pumpkins gathered
The squirrel is busy, the leaves are falling.
Winters howl on its way, the snowy
Drifts, the icy breath.

Fragile mortality questions death,
God waits a greeting on heaven's step.
Do not weep what sadness befall,
The old mans with God—after all.

First Love

When in his silvery age of time
He thinks back in melancholy to youth and first love
When the soul transcends the heart to immortality.
There resides youth the child of God.

When the private, tender, celestial relation of one to one
 Becomes the enchantment of life . . .
The delicious fancies of youth reject
The order of mature philosophy.
There is first love.

Thus, nature blooms in vivid form
The song of bird's sweeter, color of flowers deeper.
 His love breathes the fragrance of spring
Virtue sacred, passion breathless, beauty to be touched
Yet held in reverent respect.
There is first love.

This rapture from heaven holds only the tender age,
Thus he dreams back to that exquisite moment . . .
Her soft, slender hand encloses on his
Her head rests upon his shoulder.
There is first love.

Sadly, this ecstasy of love in the springtime of life
Fades with aging heart to faint memory.
He searches the eternal soul for vision before . . . his day is
        done.
There, in the far horizon of mind . . .
First love lives on in the warming rays of life's setting sun.

For God to See

O that words flow
Across this naked page, from secret
Heart to pen. Pour forth my soul
This darkened night as token left
More honoring be.

Yet in beating chambers within proud heart,
Images tease this aging mind, cling
Defiant to my quest, to fade and
Drift in endless tide.

Thus I stress this moonless night,
Exercise these fleeting thoughts
To loose the mind of cloistered
Dreams that they may come to light.

Restless sleep assails my labored senses,
Benedictions of night hold vigil o're
Shadowy visions, dream unfold the
Treasure hidden, to die unrevealed
With morning's gray dawn.

Sorry words address on this crumpled paper,
Hold what wistful wisdom left for me,
Pray thoughts not blessed to write,
Sanguinely remain for God to see.

Gift of Love

We live at the edge of silence
Having supped the feast of wonder
The glory of Gods' shining nature
Amid the pristine sunlit shadows of wilderness.

This splendor offered as a gift of love
Love carried over when silence is ours
May it live on for generations to come
Our peaceful spirit watching o'er.

Lives in the sound of calling loons,
The song of birds, the shading trees
The island view from cabin door
Bright stars that light the lakes dark shore.

In silent left a place God dwells
For in the hush of moon glow night
You feel his presence within pure air
Reach out and touch him—God is there.

God's Face

Oh! Heavenly Host of boundless love,
To whom I pray for daily bread,
To whom I beg God's special grace,
That one day I behold his face.

I sense God's spirit with setting sun,
While choirs of birds sing praise of day,
Await the coming morning dawn,
As nature's sweet alarm to pray.

The light that glitters on evening lake,
The chanting of the loon,
Echoes a higher grace and hope,
Reflected by the moon.

I wonder to God's countenance,
His glorious spirit holds,
What shining image to behold,
God's endless love unfolds.

My father kneeling at his bed,
In deep and solemn prayer,
This good man paused, smiled up at me.
The face of God was there.

In The Arms of Spring

Spring, spring is here! Wake up!
Listen, buds are popping, leaves unfold
New life on sleepy barren winter trees, the sun
Beams warmer as birds in chorus cheer.

Blue birds tune up for summer concertos.
Turtles bury their eggs amid buzzing bees,
Geese herd their young out of harms way
Bear cubs test their skill climbing trees.

The world in bright colors, breezes fresh
Perfume, beg adventure as young Lexi
And Luke clasp hands and stroll with the sounds
Of nature, into the arms of a cabin spring.

Lady of the North

There is a secret I must disclose,
A love I feel I need confess,
To spouse and family, that all may know
This fervent love and happiness.

I share a mistress with my wife,
Far beyond the city lights
She Beckons me to piney woods—
Crystal lakes, moonlit nights.

To see her splendor, know her grace—
Features that reflect her face—
A misty presence in the air,
Gently whispers she is there.

I run my fingers thru the air,
And swear I touch her sunlit hair—
Resting on my cabin deck,
I find her perfume lingers there.

She's all the seasons,
More so spring and fall—
Spring when eagerly we join in heart,
And fall when sadly again we part.

The day my soul from me departs,
My body lowered into God's sweet earth,
Perhaps wind would wail, thunder roar,
Rain pour, lightning crack,
The call of the loons no more.

Oh! That she call the sun to rise,
Dry the tear soaked leaves—
Lift the drooping blossomed flowers,
That nature no longer grieve.

Arise my spirit to join with hers,
Awaiting at my cabin door.
That I may linger at her side
This wonderous lady, I adore.

Lamb of God

We are borne as little lambs,
Lambs of God and become his sheep.
Some of us poor little lambs,
May have lost our way.

Others perhaps become little
Black sheep, and have gone
Astray. They cry Baa! Baa! To
Seek help to find their way.

These little lambs, now look to
Their shepherd, ask guidance.
They lift their heads and
Look to Jesus, shepherd and mercy.

We are all lambs of God.
Lambs that become good sheep, pray!
We must look to our shepherd—our
Shepherd Jesus for grace and mercy,
And one day pray, His heaven and peace.

Life

What fiat imposed?
What prose disposed?
What prosody? Heaven knows
What destiny? God doth show.

Life's Mystery

He walks with cane his cabin trail
His stride now slowed with purpose strolls,
Looks ahead and on either side
Perhaps some nature to unveil.

Not alone he walks the road
A lonely soft breeze follows him
It gently sways the treetops high
Ripples the grass beneath his sky.

The breeze continues as with a sigh
Following, following his every turn
So close he thought he felt its breath
Not touching him, but so close by.

He cannot guess the reason be
Or what the breeze is telling he
A lonely whisper in his ear
God is here, life's mystery near.

Long Shadows

My life has entered the long shadows of time.
The reaching arms of twilight, close out the final rays of day.
Yet these last blessed moments are brilliant with
Vivid hues of color, sunlight strewn across green grass,
Sparkling blue ponds, contrasting the dark
Shadows cast in its path.

Such are my days, warmed as though this sun
Kindled thoughts of cherished past and sweeter
Days of vibrant youth and love.

Though my steps may falter and memory
Hides in recesses of the mind, the slowing of spirit
Still profits. Thus, I stand observing my
Reflection, in long shadows on this close of day,
To pause and whisper an Ave, life is good—life is precious.

Lost Culture

He lives in an old Aquinas world,
The solemnity of Holy Mass.
The silence for introspect and prayer
The magnificence of sacred music,
With great hosannas ring. The
Bowed heads before flickering vigils
And the traces of incense there.

He withdraws from mediocrity,
The clashing sounds conjured as music—
The trash of modern art and literature,
Searches the culture lost centuries past
As solace for the soul.

There may be such as he
Where age condemns him out of touch.
Yet few offend or more suffering see,
Great culture lost more lonely be.

Lovely Memory

I must write every day,
Melancholy thoughts taunt me,
Thoughts of days gone by,
Days of joy, bright with love.

A beautiful melody, a lovely rose,
All remind me of you; thoughts
That tug the heart,
The shadow of your laughter.

A lady that was always up,
Never down, always positive, never
Sad. She was like a dream. A
Dream that should never awake.

Sadly this dream did wake. A
Dream that found the harsh light
Of day. The dream and she was gone.
Leaving me alone, alone with
Only her memory—sad but lovely.

Me and I

Pondering myself with I and me,
To find oft times we disagree.
Where I in literature, music, art,
Discover a seemingly poetic heart.

Where as me, just me, a quiet soul,
A dreamer, thinker, to some
Seem slow
A child and man few people know.

The chords of Bach in variations,
The civil War its occupation.
Dylan Thomas psalms on death,
Plato, Homer, Socrates, Goethe
All these I prize and find release.
To study, listen, providing peace.

Yet me, poor me, still
Wonders why, my weary song
Remains unheard. Tis then
My heart accepted I. A lovely
Aria heard on high.

Melancholy Night

What craft contained in thoughts
I write this late sullen hour,
While lightning streaks to light
This dark night sky.

The children lie abed with all
Their dreams and future years ahead,
I struggle to summon the morning light.

Not for wealth or laurels I write,
While distant thunder drums a melancholy beat,
To stir my aging heart, or
For the ever expounding artless critics.

But for my sacred love, the children,
Who discover my most secret heart,
And what craft unheeded save,
Attend beyond my silent grave.

Memories Weep

He's old and memories are all
That's left for him.
Memories that stir the heart, yet
Others that fall softly on the soul,
All weep.

Yes they weep recalling youth,
Where is that strong navy recruit?
The young Romeo that charmed
Pretty girls? Soulful memories are left to weep.

For now they are all gone
All distant memories, all except
One, one that remains young in
Heart, yet her memory weeps, still
A tearful smile that keeps.

Mocking Bird

While standing at my patio door,
A bel-canto voice not heard before.
Flute like trills, warbles and chirps
Compositions, harmonies, symphony exerts.

Compare to Chopin—melancholy notes.
Majestic Beethoven on breezes floats.

Yet this concert outside my door
Surpasses all music heard before
The songful word of a Mocking bird.

My Children's Grandfather

A shield of modesty his genius veiled
Vanity cloaked in humble presence,
His prayers beg no prideful
Lust or pompous airs.

A much used path where books are lent,
His late night hours in study,
Philospht, history, poetry, art,
His erudite mind concealed from us,
Love, direction, example, the obvious clues.

No formal schooling extol his craft.
With quiet talent, leads voices in Mozart, Bach,
Schubert, Handel.
Each note directed and sent high
To the honor and Glory of God.

His startling genius takes many venues,
Directing and producing theater of Ibsen,
Tennessee Williams or Charles Dickens.
Withholds his name from applauding patrons.

Each night at bedside kneeling, bows
His noble head, prayers rise on seraph's wing,
Soar above celestial stars,
To gently catch the ear of God.

More than fifty springs and winters past
In sacred ground he lies. While choirs of
Blue birds in joyful hymns above
His tomb in prayers sing.

Years of rising sun and falling shadows,
Natures flowers adorn his grave.
Memory recalls an unusual man,

Genius divinely wrought, for most a
Grandfather unrevealed and
Others sadly forgot.

Yet for you, his children,
He looks down and smiles.
Prays the angels guide you safely,
And perhaps for just a moment,
You pause, and remember him,
If only once in a while.

My Prayer

Oh light that reveals the sacred truth
Oh light that stimulates true faith
Oh light that awakens the Holy Spirit
Oh Light that glows from thee
Oh light of Christ shine on me.

Navy Corpsman WWII

Death stands waiting in harbor ships,
Death arrived with our wounded and walks
Amid the bloody terror. He stops to
Peer at gasping lives and impassively
Listens to parting prayers. "Our Father
Who art in Heaven."

Cries for help! Water! Mother! Going home?
Chills, fever. Missing limbs, lost sight,
Bloodied face, medic hurry—corpsman
Over here! "Hail Mary full of Grace."

Plug the plasma in—cleanse open
Gaping wounds. Apply the sulfa compress
Fast. Hemostats, sutures, still the pain.
Morphine, more morphine, fear,
Comforting words, prayer. While towering
Deaths shadow cast. "Lord have mercy—may
Their young lives last."

Death grins at me while selecting from
The silenced breath. Helps pull the
Blanket ore their heads—prepares the
Bags to send the dead. "Memento Mori"
His message read. "Pray for us now and at
The hour of death."

Now in my gray hairs, half a century past.
I salute the rows of stark white crosses
Where comrades whisper from
Earth beneath—"go tell the people,
Who pass us by, that here for your freedom,
Flag and country lie."

As for me—no hero am I.

My ship in peaceful waters lay,
Yet privileged that for some—
Held death at bay.
And for others can proudly kneel to pray.

Navy Humor

There are rules in military to obey,
In Navy or Marines you never delay.
Salute your superiors every day,
March in formation in line you pray.
Manual of arms prepare to display,
Risk your life for government pay.
But never, oh never be such a dope,
In community shower—you drop the soap.

Ode to Old Age

The golden years of wisdom and grace greet
The arrival of winter's chill. Intellect
In tandem with aching bones, plod
The snowy scene, yet gracefully accept
The wounds of extended life.
Philosophy and faith displace the fear
Of approaching death.

Reconcile the spring of life is gone,
Lost in the haze of lazy summer days.
Now the howl of stormy winds prevail,
A journey into winter's blast.
While o're the shoulder of mind,
Visions of youth fade.

A cold white moon peers through frosted
Window panes. Lights I pray a noble past.
No need to brace against the clock of life,
The race is run, a time to pause,
Think back to gentle days of love and youth.

Spring will come, the sun will rise,
Warm rains will thaw the winter's chill.
Song birds will sing, the loon will call,
The glory of God's world is here—after all.

Ode to Septic (Tank)

Fear not the waste thou dost dispose—
The quantity we should never know,
Or peril befalling the tank below—
Care not how long for your release,
Read, (we pray not *War and Peace*).

Yet through it all, your soulful caper,
Keep in mind the loathsome paper.
The smallest sheet may e'er suffice—
Excess use can mean a price.

So, extra pulls of paper, please,
For blowing nose, perhaps a sneeze—
Or just the extra insuring wipes—
Choose the basket, save our pipes!

P.S.
No Kleenex
No Tampax
No Condoms
No Complaints

Our Home and Family

The beautiful Rice Creek flows
Quietly and gracefully, edging
The back yard. This splendor was
Our daily gift of nature.

Exotic birds, the crane and
Others frequent its waters. Offering
A rare and lovely sight.

This is the brook I strived to
Build her home next to. This
Brook, longside a garden of flowers
At which to look, their petals bloom of love.

Our home reflected in its waters.
Stirs beautiful thoughts and memories.
Five striking children silhouetted
In this lovely background.

Leaves an old man holding back tears,
Tear drops that produce vivid
Mental pictures of bride and little ones.
Now grown with memories of their own.
The bride now with God, watching ore.

Our Life and Home

To look back on 86 years—
I see a rich life, wondrous love.
My eyes reveal a lovely lady—
All one could ask, a perfect wife.

A beautiful home alongside a creek—
Its' features reflected in its silvery waters.
A yard to dream of caresses the creek bank.
There a garden of flowers at which to look.

All blessed by heaven's love and beauty.
Five lovely children silhouetted in
This enchanting background,
Four stunning daughters, one handsome son.

God has blessed our family profoundly.
Blessings, I offer thanks for daily.
Blessings of love, affection and faith.
I look to heaven and thank my Mary
Also, for her astounding contribution and love.

Our Rice Creek

The beautiful stream like heaven's
Waters, flows gently, caressing the
Banks on which I stand. Her bountiful
Stream, ripples like her wind blown
Hair.

She is lovely to watch, as I stand on
Her golden enchanting banks. She
Speaks to me softly with lapping
Rivulets of motion, telling me to stay
Do not leave me.

I would never leave her, she was such a
Part of me. I watch from my window,
As she beckons me, "come see the rare
And wondrous crane standing in the stream."

I choke up as we prepare to leave.
My daughter sitting near her banks sheds
Tears. I hold her hand as we take one
Last tearful look and farewell to this
Love, this gracious queen, our Rice Creek.

Poet's Lament

As an unacknowledged legislator
To the world,
I submit what craft to lend,
Art unheeded save, attend
Beyond the silent grave.

Life's poetic thoughts distilled,
Filed in cloistered memory lost,
Vintage unsavored, words muffled
Away in dusty bin.

Remain secret from the
Gilded halls of fame.
Pray some glimpse of character
And heart, bring sanguine closure
To my craft or art.

Poets Heart

There breeds a soul within his heart,
Where sun rise lingers longer,
The color deeper in summer sky,
The music of birds while circling high.

Ask the sun, the stars, the moon,
The lonely call of distant loon,
Ask if you hear or sight enhance
Or pass the scene with careless glance?

The poets prose paints words to lite—
The starry night, the moons soft glow,
The rising sun, the chanting loon,
The song of birds in joyful flight.

The melancholy of setting sun,
The racing moon when day is done,
The silence creeping to your door
The lapping sounds of waves on shore.

The poets heart sails on a star,
Surveys the untold grief below,
The tears that streak the fragile soul,
Of shattered dreams, lost love to die,
Like withered blossoms from the sky.

Return in Spring

The old man, deep in thought
,Sat overlooking the cabin lake,
Where half a century spent his summers,
Now sadly preparing to leave.
The chill of winter not far behind,
He ponders the long weary journey south.

Breathing in the autumnal fall air,
Bright sun filtering thru bony tree branches,
The few remaining yellow leaves drift softly down,
Gathering about his feet.

Reconciles his life as in the yellow leaf of time,
Looks to his final days,
With spouse and children close to his aging heart.
With them natures beauty comes alive.
God's love fills his soul.

A lonesome call resounds on the still lake.
The man looks to find a loon too aged to travel south.
The bird bids a melodic farewell,
As though to wish him well.

His love for the loon compels him to descend the steep hill.
The loon greets him with flapping wings.
With labored breath the old man urges his friend to fly!
Fly south again that you may sing and pray we both return in
        spring.

Sacred Years

He earned a pompous side
A singular elitist, a shielded vise.
A moving experience, a meditation
Unshared leaves a lonely man.

Oh! To share a Shakespeare sonnet
A Chopin nocturne, a Mozart concerto,
Beethoven's 5th—Vivaldi's Gloria
Opera tenors—be canto sopranos.

Writing of Henry Adams,
Montaigne, Voltaire, Goethe
Poetry of Dickinson, Milton
Dylan Thomas, prose of Cervantes.

Yet lonely heart and all
Attending solitude aside
The urge to share joys and tears
Give thanks, God blessed his sacred years.

Share Sadness

Give not your grief to just one—
Spare a portion for despair to come—
Reserve tears, agony, sullen hours
For these.

Prepare if you can, the ultimate test—
A tiny form asleep in quiet grave.
Unrelenting pain—grief so deep
Your senses dull—you silently weep.

Save some tears if you can.
I have no grief to part.
I lost a child—my little girl
And with her lost my heart.

Special Angel of Heaven

When you my angel left—left to fly
With angels of heaven, you left my world,
Leaving me alone. Alone with my
Tender thoughts of you.

You would never leave me. We were
So in love. Your presence with me
No more. Your smile and small hand
In mine no more. God called, my love was gone.

My heart is broken. I can't deny
God's Holy will. God knows your
Lovely soul and gracious heart. God in His
Great love chose you, chose you for His
Special angel of heaven.

Stairway to Heaven

"Hail Mary full of Grace
The Lord is with thee."
Yet my parish and many others she is not.
Not in prayers, not in sermon, or images.

"Blessed art thou among women
And blessed is the fruit of your womb Jesus."
Yet we ignore this Glorious lady
Our strongest connection to Christ.

For most of us she builds faith.
Her wondrous love and daily guidance,
Build faith, solid as stone
It goes into the depths of our nature.

For some the foundation, blood of life,
A tendency to devotion, sacrifice and
Struggles. These stones of faith are placed
On the alter stairs, accumulate and form a
Stairway to God—
Our Blessed Mother is with Him.

Ave Maria

Star Dust

Listening to Glen Gould play the
Goldberg Variations, sends me on a
Nostalgic trip to the days of love
And youth.

Days rooted in memories,
Pleasant thoughts of you
My love. cherished years
Of affection, borne of God.

I hold your hand, your small
Hand in mine, your soft grip
Holds my heart. The moon blinks,
Stars fall, their dust finds my eyes.

Dust that awakens the precious
Truth, a wonderful life, a beautiful
Wife, extraordinary children all,
To enrich my days and remaining time.

Dust that brings tears, soulful thoughts
Filled with memories lost. Old age
Leaves painful, yet tender recall of
Wonderous years, thus, dry your tears.

The Grandeur of God

The sky, moon and stars in harmony,
Roof the splendor of the cabin lake,
Millions of stars showcase the over flowing big dipper,
Pouring forth goblets of ethereal moonshine,
Inebriating senses, cheering the heart.

Natures stage is set, the owl hoots a final call,
The moon's golden reflection leads to my
Open bedroom window. The epic unfolds.
A chorus of loons prelude with Gregorian
Chant of evening prayers.

Bull frogs provide a background of cellos.
A soft breeze sweeps the tree tops like
A bow on strings of a violin. A lone wolf's
Howl accompanies the nights stellar
Performance with a haunting solo. The
Lake softly laps the shore in relaxing
Rhythm.

Pure night air, enchanting nocturnes, blissfully
Lull you to sleep. Song birds awaken to
First light. Sun breaks the morning gray,
With quivers of blazing color, rising
Above tree tops, painting the lake
A crimson hue. Thus the earth
Rejoices in the grandeur of God,
Greeting the new day.

The Terror On Cabin Road

Safely you rest on the cabin deck,
Brandy and cigar close at hand,
Away from the horror on cabin road,
The lines been drawn in the sand.

You drowse as boats go cruising by,
The sun is high in summer sky,
There's talk of walking to the bridge,
To see bear and deer, where eagles fly.

The threat of what may cross you path,
The monster that awaits you there,
In holding pattern circles the road,
The human carnage yet untold.

Prepare for combat, full metal jacket,
Camouflage if you can,
Think positive, you will not die,
Search and destroy, the black deer fly.

The Volunteer

You never know how much to give . . .
Until you're called to rise.
'Tis when your very image grows
To reach the starry skies.

For with every act of kindness
You touch the robe of Christ.
So, grab the torch and volunteer
And pray your toil sufficed.

That this kind service for love of God
The effort for your soul
Recorded on the books of Peter
Should be your saving goal.

Today I'm Seventy-Seven

The old man sat in the bright morning sun,
The trees in glorious color
Mindful of Christmas in October.
Leaves drifting about his lake cabin
Like the snow of winter,
Send a moments chill through his aged body.
He looks up at the blue sky of heaven
Not yet dear Lord, today I'm seventy-seven.

Tower Bells Ring

Sadly thoughts of death hold sway
As attending years dominion plays
Unsure life held in rigid soul
Awaits the tower bells toll.

Death looms over fragile breath
Mortality questions the final rest
For surely no one ever dies
As Jesus lives, the soul survives.

Some shall mourn the body gone
Weep with eulogy, casket and song.
The soul in heaven watches o're
Thru celestial windows, God's open door.

All things subsist and do not die
As nature conceals itself in fall,
Revealed again in spring.
The soul like nature, remains to live,
Heedless of the tower bell's ring.

Truth

In the tangled deep dark forest
Of the mind, truth resides in total
Isolation. Revealing light fails,
Only truths promising shadow
Or doubt prevails.

Where erudite and professorial minds shun
The fearsome truth, simple souls
Heedless of its impact, content
Themselves in the daily pabulum of discourse.

Yet in the deep forests, it springs forth
As lovely blossomed flowers, beckoning
The curious mind to pluck its blooms,
Only to droop and wilt in compromised thought.

Should that truth sound from lips,
The resultant tornadic winds would scatter
And disperse weak kneed values so
Piously held—revealing a sordid misguided world.

Hope, clinging to a simple truth,
A life line to grasp the greater light,
As the mornings suns glow
Awaken a new dawn.

Man shall walk in a new day,
A holy sight, a blessed thing,
And the prophet of 2000 years,
Will smile to behold such a lovely light.

Waiting Heaven

Our lives reached the time of winter,
Accompanying yellow leaf buried
'Neath the crusty snows of age.

Once vigorous days, now slowed
To hesitating breath.
Vision dimmed, ergo struggle
To read cherished thoughts of genius.

Our springs of life, summers, winters past
Like fleeting misty memories.
Still we have each other, thus can sing
My Mary, our love, God and waiting heaven.

Waste Not

The search for knowledge in various places,
Education's source where no one traces.
The jewels uncovered with thoughtful
Elan, often revealed while on the john.
Thus natures calls never forsook, attend thy visit with
Scholarly book.

Welcome Peace

She dare not close her eyes
For death stood by her bed.
She dare not doze or sleep
For fear life's spirit fled.

A man of God stopped by,
His voice was soft and kind.
God's great words of love were said.
Sacred oils on hands were spread,
A cross of oil upon her head.

Then placed the body of Christ
Upon her feverish tongue.
She closed her eyes in welcome peace
Her toil on earth was done.

On the death of his sister Kay, age 86

When We Met

A beautiful vision in starched crisp white,
A colored ribbon arranged just right,
An angel of mercy blessed on high,
The girl I'll love 'til the day I die.

Happy Valentine's Day!
Love, Ken

Who is She?

The less traveled cabin road aged along with him,
Towering pines leave precious view of the
Deep blue sky. This shaded pristine path
Edged with wild roses and splashed with
Bouquets of Black-eyed Susans, is where
He daily walks.

A bluff overlooking a crystal clear lake,
An overview on nature's grandeur,
Sheltered by surrounding verdant forest,
Give glimpse to the old man's cabin.
Thankful on his return she is there.

A mystic maiden of golden hair,
A garland of flowers round her waist,
Blue birds and finches in the air, nature's
Beauty in her smile, she welcomes
Him to rest awhile.

She is with him when lake loons call,
She's with the doe and fawn on cabin road.
She guides him from path of bear,
Rejoices he had seen them there.

She awakens him in starry sleep,
To hear the wonderous sounds of night.
The loons performing LaBoheme, raccoons
In comic noisy fight, prowl the
Trees to his delight.

Ask her name, the spell on him,
This lovely maiden with golden hair?
She is the sun, the wind, the thunder and rain,
The trees that bud, the flowering glade.
Tell them as you go forth—
She is the spirit of the North.

Winter Prayer

Spring has whispered her coming,
Yet today, snow flakes gently fall.
No sound, no threat, just gently and
Easy falling, they spire and dance
As they tumble down.

Great winter bids a final farewell.
He tucked winter away, he invites
The sun to warm beams and prays
His friends reduce the snow banks
To gentle streams.

His frosty face is kinder, more pleasing,
Beckons the coming spring to dull
The coughing and sneezing, allowing
Time to store the toys of winter games.

Good bye to winter sports and hello
To spring and her soft breezes,
Special cheer for the magic month of
May with her brilliant flowers blossoming.

Good bye to winter sports and hello to
Spring and her merry gladness.
Warming sun and greening grasses,
Opening lakes and tanning lasses.

With God

As the twilight of life dims
Life's sequel begins with old age.
The past like shadows cross the mind,
Some dark with agony—others bright as morning sun.

Gives pause to ponder the inevitable.
Should I choose, it would be spring or fall.
Spring when the earth returns to life,
Fall when nature prepares to sleep.

Would that my farewell display dignity,
A calm adieu, a clasp of hands,
A furtive tear, kind words, and
Welcoming angels around my bed.

My friend Christ arrives to take me.
Thus the sun will rise, birds sing vespers,
Flowers bloom. Where I lie new grass and sod
No need to weep, for I'm with God.

You Are Here

Old age breeds a lonely heart,
Lost yesterdays, lost romance.
Lost are hours with you.
Lost is laughter and joy.

I retreat to my quiet room,
I think of our lovely past,
Your beautiful smile and touch
Of your hand in mine, never to return.

I feel your closeness and know
You are with me. With me as always,
As in our beautiful past.

Alas! I fight tears, as thoughts are the
Arms that caress me, so near that I
Breathe your perfume in. I reach to
Touch you and know you are here.

Young Man Grown Old

I am if you run the tests
Follow what my heart proclaims
I am if revealed or told
A young man grown old.

Who thrashes thru the web of years
As clouds lie heavy on labored breast
The sun of youth faith memory peaks
As thoughts arise but fail the test

I search a hill above dark clouds
Where grass is green and sun rays beam
A place to rest my love and I
The years pass by in cloudless sky

Our days reviewed in heavenly blue
With ribbon bows on years of yore
With each a prize our love is told
For her a young man grown old

Your Well

What grace that flows from pen
To paper? Are the nuggets of gold
Diction of your well? The cool and
Refreshing water that pours from the
Soul.

Water to strengthen faith, the love
Of God, renew the ties to family
And provides the confidence to
Carry on a noble life.

Washes away the great bond
That holds you helpless and depressed.
Thus, this water of your well, wipes
Away the fears and torments of this life.

You have only to drink from it!
Your well will lead you from
The Darkness to glorious light.

About the Author

Kenneth P. Firnstahl was born in Long Prarie, MN to Otto and Cecelia Firnstahl in 1924, the second youngest of seven. He grew up in rural Minnesota working in his family's grocery store. At age 18 he enlisted in the military and served as a Navy corpsman during WWII. After, he attended the University of Minnesota and built a career in the broadcasting business. He met Mary Louise Haas while she was working as an RN at St. Mary's hospital in Minneapolis, and they were married in 1949. Ken and Mary raised 5 children in Fridley, Minnesota. After retirement, they spent winters in Arizona and summers at the beloved family cabin. Throughout his life, Ken loved his family and his friends. He loved literature, listening to music, and the call of a loon. And he always enjoyed a good bottle of wine with a cigar. Mary passed away in 2009, Ken in 2015.

www.ingramcontent.com/pod-product-compliance
Lightning Source LLC
Chambersburg PA
CBHW041205150726